The Book of Ecclesiastes

K.W. Bow

Copyright 2016 by Kenneth W. Bow
The book author retains sole copyright to
his contributions to this book.
Published 2016.
Printed in the United States of America.

All rights reserved.

No portion of this book may be reproduced, stored in a retrieval system, or transmitted in any form or by any means – electronic, mechanical, photocopy, recording, scanning, or other – except for brief quotations in critical reviews or articles, without the prior written permission of the author.

ISBN 978-1-9860028-6-1

Front cover design by Mark Gauthier.

This book was published by BookCrafters,
Parker, Colorado.
bookcrafterscolorado@gmail.com

This book may be ordered from
www.bookcrafters.net and other online bookstores.

Foreword

Thank you reader, for selecting my book. There are many choices of books and we all have a limited window of time to read. I appreciate you purchasing my product. It is a humbling thing to know someone would choose to purchase, and then read your work. I do not take it as a small matter. By purchasing and reading a book, the reader and the author form a certain bond as they travel a road together for a short time. It is especially rewarding when the two agree on the content. It is my hope you can find inspiration and life challenges in the pages of this small booklet.

From the days of my high school years I have found the Bible fascinating. I have travelled to Israel on two occasions to learn more about the land and culture of the Bible. I worked on an archaeological dig and lived on a Kibbutz to better inform myself of how to understand this book from God. I have read it from cover to cover over twenty times, and it is still as exciting to me as it ever was.

The Bible is a magnificent journey and experience. It is ever a delight. In it you will travel to distant lands and meet some of the most incredible people of history.

It will introduce you to kings and peasants. You will walk the palace halls of castles and the open fields of the countryside. You will meet the famous and be introduced to people whose name we will never know. You will read some of the greatest love stories ever told and you will see the dark side of man as the evil manifests itself in heinous ways. Every emotion of man is highlighted at some time. You will see greed and avarice and murderous covetousness. You will also see the greatest examples of love and sacrifice that mankind has ever contributed. For indeed the Bible is the story of man. It is the whole story, and nothing is left out or omitted. It is the ultimate mirror of life.

When we invest time in the Bible we indulge a bit of the eternal. The Bible will never pass away, even in the eons of the future. If you have read it sincerely then my hope is this small work will intensify your understanding and enjoyment a little more. It is the grandest journey we can make while in this life. Thank you for sharing a portion of your life journey with me.

Kenneth Bow

The Book of Ecclesiastes

Author: Solomon

Date: Tenth Century BC

Theme: The vanity of life

Each of the books included in the sacred Canon are unique. This holds true of Ecclesiastes in a special way. Solomon wrote three books in the Bible. He wrote the Song of Solomon while he was young and had only sixty wives and eighty concubines. In his middle years of life he wrote Proverbs, which is a contrast between two women. One woman is the woman of the street, the seductress. The other woman is Lady Wisdom. Then in his fading years of life, he wrote this book, Ecclesiastes. At the end of his life he had seven hundred wives and three hundred concubines. He had written one thousand five songs and three thousand proverbs. Ecclesiastes has been called the Sphinx of the Bible, for it is grave, majestic, and mysterious.

Ecclesiastes is unique in sacred Canon. Luke wrote his gospel and the sequel, the book of Acts. John wrote his gospel and his triad of books, and Revelation. The

Apostle Paul wrote for a period of about a decade. Only Solomon wrote books in various stages of life that reflect the changing viewpoint of one man's life. This, the final book of his life, shows the transition of youth to age. Ecclesiastes is the contrast of youthful dreams to the realization we will all face death and judgment. It is the *Hebel* of life. Life on earth is empty, transitory, and unsatisfactory.

The Bible is many things, including philosophy. Nowhere is philosophy more on display than in this grand book. The author saw all life had to offer and concluded it is *Hebel*, empty. At the end of all conclusions, all that matters is God. No man on earth was better qualified to write this perspective than Solomon. God Himself acknowledged Solomon as the wisest man to ever live. He was the richest man on earth during his reign in Jerusalem. His life is without sequel.

Solomon is not a bitter old man as some might present him. He is not disillusioned. He is a man who has seen more, and experienced more, than any man in history. From his coronation in Gibeon decades before, until this writing, he is the single most qualified man to write on the journey of life. Far from bitter, he is a clear eyed visionary putting the most important subject of every life on planet earth to words of eternal wisdom.

When he concludes his treatise in the final chapter, his deductions are overwhelming, convincing, and eternal. ***Fear God and keep His commandments, this is the whole duty of man, for God shall bring every work into judgment.***

Chapter 1

1.1 The words of the Preacher, the son of David, king in Jerusalem.

1. The preacher. One who addresses an assembly. The son of David, hence Solomon.

1.2 Vanity of vanities, saith the Preacher, vanity of vanities; all is vanity.

1.2 Vanity. This is the key word and the theme of the entire book. The Hebrew word *hebel*, has been translated many ways, by numerous people. Some meanings have been futility, emptiness, nothingness, and even absurdity. The general gist is that it encompasses no value or profit. It speaks of things transitory or that pass away. The *Qoheleth*, or preacher, is not saying there is no value in temporal things. He is stating that after a lifetime of living, and seeing many things, all of it is of no value in eternity. The author is speaking of things under the sun, which are temporal things. The casting of vanity over life does not include the fear of God, or even enjoying life. He is simply saying the pursuit of these things is *hebel*, or vain.

1.3 What profit hath a man of all his labour which he taketh under the sun?
1.3 What profit? The question is what eternal profit? The term under the sun, is used twenty nine times in the book. This term identifies the temporal world.

1.4-11 One generation passeth away, and another generation cometh: but the earth abideth for ever. 5 The sun also ariseth, and the sun goeth down, and hasteth to his place where he arose.
6 The wind goeth toward the south, and turneth about unto the north; it whirleth about continually, and the wind returneth again according to his circuits. 7 All the rivers run into the sea; yet the sea is not full; unto the place from whence the rivers come, thither they return again. 8 All things are full of labour; man cannot utter it: the eye is not satisfied with seeing, nor the ear filled with hearing. 9 The thing that hath been, it is that which shall be; and that which is done is that which shall be done: and there is no new thing under the sun. 10 Is there any thing whereof it may be said, See, this is new? it hath been already of old time, which was before us. 11 There is no remembrance of former things; neither shall there be any remembrance of things that are to come with those that shall come after.

1.4-11 The cycles of nature testify of this concept of *hebel*. Nature goes on and on, but man, the diadem of God's creation passes away. This opening observation is the overall canopy of the book.

1.12-18 I the Preacher was king over Israel in Jerusalem. 13 And I gave my heart to seek and search out by wisdom concerning all things that are done under

heaven: this sore travail hath God given to the sons of man to be exercised therewith. 14 I have seen all the works that are done under the sun; and, behold, all is vanity and vexation of spirit. 15 That which is crooked cannot be made straight: and that which is wanting cannot be numbered. 16 I communed with mine own heart, saying, Lo, I am come to great estate, and have gotten more wisdom than all they that have been before me in Jerusalem: yea, my heart had great experience of wisdom and knowledge. 17 And I gave my heart to know wisdom, and to know madness and folly: I perceived that this also is vexation of spirit. 18 For in much wisdom is much grief: and he that increaseth knowledge increaseth sorrow.

1.12-18 Solomon. No other person in history is more qualified than Solomon to make these conclusions. God used Solomon's earthly successes to speak to the world about hebel, or vanity. Seven times in this writing Solomon says it is vexation of spirit. He is stating the obvious conclusion that this world, and all it can give as a reward, is futility. Solomon's great wisdom did not unlock life's ultimate questions. Solomon's former book, the book of Proverbs, emphasizes the benefits of wisdom. In the closing years of his life he acknowledges wisdom has limitations. This book is the summum bonum, the quest for the chief good of life.

Chapter 2

2.1-11 I said in mine heart, Go to now, I will prove thee with mirth, therefore enjoy pleasure: and, behold, this also is vanity. 2 I said of laughter, It is mad: and of mirth, What doeth it? 3 I sought in mine heart to give myself unto wine, yet acquainting mine heart with wisdom; and to lay hold on folly, till I might see what was that good for the sons of men, which they should do under the heaven all the days of their life. 4 I made me great works; I builded me houses; I planted me vineyards: 5 I made me gardens and orchards, and I planted trees in them of all kind of fruits: 6 I made me pools of water, to water therewith the wood that bringeth forth trees: 7 I got me servants and maidens, and had servants born in my house; also I had great possessions of great and small cattle above all that were in Jerusalem before me: 8 I gathered me also silver and gold, and the peculiar treasure of kings and of the provinces: I gat me men singers and women singers, and the delights of the sons of men, as musical instruments, and that of all sorts. 9 So I was great, and increased more than all that were before me in Jerusalem: also my wisdom remained with me. 10 And whatsoever mine eyes desired I kept not from them, I withheld not my heart from any joy;

for my heart rejoiced in all my labour: and this was my portion of all my labour. 11 Then I looked on all the works that my hands had wrought, and on the labour that I had laboured to do: and, behold, all was vanity and vexation of spirit, and there was no profit under the sun.

2.1-11 Self-indulgence. Solomon pursued many forms of escape that men continue to try today. All mankind eventually ends up at the same mountain peak of disillusion. The long list of escape methods included mirth (pleasure or rejoicing), wine, building projects, accumulating wealth, art, gardens, orchards, trees, pools of water, servants, maidens, great herds of animals, silver, gold, choirs, and women. When he had exhausted these many attempts at lasting fulfillment and contentment, he concluded it was all *hebel*, vanity, with no lasting pleasure and fulfillment. He accrued more than any man before him. He was great in the sight of all jealous and hungry men. Every single desire of his heart was granted completely. Finally he observed it all like a world conqueror, and realized it is all just more of the same. This conclusion alone makes the book of Ecclesiastes of immense value to all people who will hear. One thousand years later the aged, frail Apostle John will echo this conclusion; *for all that is in the world, the lust of the flesh, the lust of the eyes, and the pride of life, is not of the Father, 1 Jn 2.16.*

2.12-17 And I turned myself to behold wisdom, and madness, and folly: for what can the man do that cometh after the king? even that which hath been already done. 13 Then I saw that wisdom excelleth folly, as far as light excelleth darkness. 14 The wise man's eyes are in his head; but the fool walketh in

darkness: and I myself perceived also that one event happeneth to them all. 15 Then said I in my heart, As it happeneth to the fool, so it happeneth even to me; and why was I then more wise? Then I said in my heart, that this also is vanity. 16 For there is no remembrance of the wise more than of the fool for ever; seeing that which now is in the days to come shall all be forgotten. And how dieth the wise man? as the fool. 17 Therefore I hated life; because the work that is wrought under the sun is grievous unto me: for all is vanity and vexation of spirit.

2.12-17 Wisdom. Solomon now records his observation of the intangibles. He lays wisdom and folly side by side. He records that wisdom does indeed exceed folly (foolishness). Then he observes that neither survives the death all men must face. Wisdom is helpful and all men should desire it, but ultimately even wisdom decays into *hebel*, vanity. This conclusion also is of great benefit to any who will harken. All Solomon had accrued in his life would be left to someone else. The only things that survive the grave are the things God instructs us to possess.

2.18-26 Yea, I hated all my labour which I had taken under the sun: because I should leave it unto the man that shall be after me. 19 And who knoweth whether he shall be a wise man or a fool? yet shall he have rule over all my labour wherein I have laboured, and wherein I have shewed myself wise under the sun. This is also vanity. 20 Therefore I went about to cause my heart to despair of all the labour which I took under the sun. 21 For there is a man whose labour is in wisdom, and in knowledge, and in equity; yet to a man that hath not laboured therein shall he leave

it for his portion. This also is vanity and a great evil. 22 For what hath man of all his labour, and of the vexation of his heart, wherein he hath laboured under the sun? 23 For all his days are sorrows, and his travail grief; yea, his heart taketh not rest in the night. This is also vanity. 24 There is nothing better for a man, than that he should eat and drink, and that he should make his soul enjoy good in his labour. This also I saw, that it was from the hand of God. 25 For who can eat, or who else can hasten hereunto, more than I? 26 For God giveth to a man that is good in his sight wisdom, and knowledge, and joy: but to the sinner he giveth travail, to gather and to heap up, that he may give to him that is good before God. This also is vanity and vexation of spirit.

2.18-26 Wisdom, more valuable than folly. Solomon concludes that even though wisdom only assists to the grave, wisdom is still a big help. The quality of life for a wise man verses the quality of life for a fool cannot be tabulated. The hours of peace and contentment verses the hours of fear and torment cannot be compared. Wisdom does stop at the grave, but the journey to the grave is immeasurably better with wisdom as your guide. All of life's accruements are passed to another, but the quality of life while on earth is not to be disdained. Several times Solomon will return to this theme in this book; enjoy life, eat and drink, be satisfied with the reward of your labor. This is what God intends for mankind while on their earthly journey. This is from the hand of God. He is not ranting or prating about life, he is saying live well and enjoy life, that is the best road.

Chapter 3

3.1-8 To every thing there is a season, and a time to every purpose under the heaven: 2 A time to be born, and a time to die; a time to plant, and a time to pluck up that which is planted; 3 A time to kill, and a time to heal; a time to break down, and a time to build up; 4 A time to weep, and a time to laugh; a time to mourn, and a time to dance; 5 A time to cast away stones, and a time to gather stones together; a time to embrace, and a time to refrain from embracing; 6 A time to get, and a time to lose; a time to keep, and a time to cast away; 7 A time to rend, and a time to sew; a time to keep silence, and a time to speak; 8 A time to love, and a time to hate; a time of war, and a time of peace.

3.1-8 The seasons. As the writer looks at the overview of life, he uses fourteen pairs of opposites to show the journey of life as a cycle in itself. This passage is a beautiful poetic piece of timeless prose. Every culture and every epoch of man can relate to this passage. While stating that nothing changes, he inserts the cycle of life that is change within no change. To gather stones and then discard stones is an apt illustration of the cycle of life. To be born, to plant, to kill, to break down, to weep, to mourn, to cast away stones, to embrace, to get, to keep, to rend, to keep silence, to love, and ultimately to war, are the shadow of every man's progressing life. And then the sunset of every life reflects, to die, to pluck up, to heal, to build up, to laugh, to dance, to gather stones, to refrain from embracing, to lose, to cast away, to sew, to speak, to hate, and finally to have peace. The stages and journey of every life can be summed up by this one poetic passage of eastern wisdom. This is the sum, the paradox, and the essence of life.

3.9-15 What profit hath he that worketh in that wherein he laboureth? 10 I have seen the travail, which God hath given to the sons of men to be exercised in it. 11 He hath made every thing beautiful in his time: also he hath set the world in their heart, so that no man can find out the work that God maketh from the beginning to the end. 12 I know that there is no good in them, but for a man to rejoice, and to do good in his life. 13 And also that every man should eat and drink, and enjoy the good of all his labour, it is the gift of God. 14 I know that, whatsoever God doeth, it shall be for ever: nothing can be put to it, nor any thing taken from it: and God doeth it, that men should fear before him. 15 That which hath been is now; and that which is to be hath already been; and God requireth that which is past.

3.9-15 The profit. The writer returns to the overview of life. Tangible things will fade in satisfaction; intangible things are temporal, so enjoy the life God gives. This is the gift of life, the gift of joy, and ultimately the gift of God to mankind. There is no profit outside this view of life. If you choose to live in this view of life, everything is beautiful. Life is an amazing discovery without limit. The ultimate is for man to rejoice and to do good in this life. To eat and to drink, and to enjoy the good of his labor, it is the gift of God. This is the cycle of life God gives to mankind. For this cause, men should fear before God. This advice to fear God will be repeated a total of six times in this book.

3.16-22 And moreover I saw under the sun the place of judgment, that wickedness was there; and the place of righteousness, that iniquity was there. 17 I said in mine heart, God shall judge the righteous and the wicked: for there is a time there for every purpose and for every work. 18 I said in mine heart concerning the estate of the sons of men, that God might manifest them, and that they might see that they themselves are beasts. 19 For that which befalleth the sons of men befalleth beasts; even one thing befalleth them: as the one dieth, so dieth the other; yea, they have all one breath; so that a man hath no preeminence above a beast: for all is vanity.20 All go unto one place; all are of the dust, and all turn to dust again. 21 Who knoweth the spirit of man that goeth upward, and the spirit of the beast that goeth downward to the earth? 22 Wherefore I perceive that there is nothing better, than that a man should rejoice in his own works; for that is his portion: for who shall bring him to see what shall be after him?

3.16-22 The eternal. The writer would be remiss if he ignored the eternal, so he turns his eye to that horizon. He examines the place of judgment. He affirms God will judge these things. Death is the great conqueror of man and beast, and every living thing. The similarity of death ends at the dust, for the spirit of man ascends, while the spirit of beasts decends. Then the cycle is again affirmed, *there is nothing better than that a man should rejoice in his own works, for that is his portion. Who shall bring him to see what shall be after him?* The Old Testament says very little about the life after death. Here Solomon openly wonders about it, but hints he believes in it when he speaks of a coming judgment. Ultimately in 12.7, he concludes the spirit of man returns to God. After enjoying this life as the gift of God, there is another life to live for.

Chapter 4

4.1-3 So I returned, and considered all the oppressions that are done under the sun: and behold the tears of such as were oppressed, and they had no comforter; and on the side of their oppressors there was power; but they had no comforter. 2 Wherefore I praised the dead which are already dead more than the living which are yet alive. 3 Yea, better is he than both they, which hath not yet been, who hath not seen the evil work that is done under the sun.

4.1-3 Injustice. Solomon leaves the heart of man and looks at the world at large. He concludes some injustices are worse than death. He muses the unborn are better than those oppressed. The word for oppression, ashuq, has to do with tyranny. Who can observe tyranny more astutely than a King himself? Ironically more lamented than the oppression, was the absence of anyone to show comfort to the oppressed. This is amazing insight for a man so insulated by worldly comforts and servants. This is a flashback to the moment he understood the Shunnamite girl who loved her shepherd, and the moment he knew who the true mother was between the two harlots. It shows great human insight into empathy.

4.4-6 Again, I considered all travail, and every right work, that for this a man is envied of his neighbour. This is also vanity and vexation of spirit. 5 The fool foldeth his hands together, and eateth his own flesh. 6 Better is an handful with quietness, than both the hands full with travail and vexation of spirit.

4.4-6 Work. He views the man who works an excessive amount in comparison to the man who works just enough to get by. In the end, both are *hebel*. It is the contentment of life that gauges the value of work and accomplishment.

4.7-8 Then I returned, and I saw vanity under the sun. 8 There is one alone, and there is not a second; yea, he hath neither child nor brother: yet is there no end of all his labour; neither is his eye satisfied with riches; neither saith he, For whom do I labour, and bereave my soul of good? This is also vanity, yea, it is a sore travail.

4.7-8 The miser. Solomon addresses the one who works alone and never stops to enjoy his labor. The miser is never satisfied with his labor, he always wants more. This causes the miser to bereave his own soul of good. This statement is an early form of the law of diminishing returns. The longer and harder the miser works, the less satisfaction he finds. It violates God's law to enjoy the fruit of your labor.

4.9-12 Two are better than one; because they have a good reward for their labour. 10 For if they fall, the one will lift up his fellow: but woe to him that is alone when he falleth; for he hath not another to help him up. 11 Again, if two lie together, then they have heat:

but how can one be warm alone? 12 And if one prevail against him, two shall withstand him; and a threefold cord is not quickly broken.

4.9-12 The value of two. The echo from Eden sounds, it is not good for man to be alone, Gen 2.18. The enjoyment of labor is doubled by the addition of another. The advantage of help by lifting your fallen companion is stated. The companionship of a mate that brings warmth, and the defense of your companion all defend Eden's echo. As Solomon's eye looks to the world, he endorses the echo of Eden.

4.13 Better is a poor and a wise child than an old and foolish king, who will no more be admonished.

4.13 Solomon's epitaph. This is the wisest man in the world enscribing his own epitaph. Infinitely better is a wise and poor child (as he was at Gibeon), than an old and foolish King (as he now was). The simple, pure days of his early kingdom now stand in contrast to a complicated court with one thousand women, and temples to many false Gods. This is truly *hebel*, vanity of vanities. No verse penned in any of his three books concisely states his life as poignantly.

4.14-16 For out of prison he cometh to reign; whereas also he that is born in his kingdom becometh poor. 15 I considered all the living which walk under the sun, with the second child that shall stand up in his stead. 16 There is no end of all the people, even of all that have been before them: they also that come after shall not rejoice in him. Surely this also is vanity and vexation of spirit.

4.14-16 Litany of *hebel*. Solomon poses that Kings come from prisons, and the privileged fall into poverty. As his eye scans all the castes of life, he remembers he is King by his father's choice. His brothers were in line for the throne, but his mother petitioned his father while his father was on his deathbed, and he, the son who was second, now resides on the throne. It underlines again the *hebel* of life. Solomon mirrors Aesop who said "our insignificance is often the cause of our safety."

Chapter 5

5.1-3 Keep thy foot when thou goest to the house of God, and be more ready to hear, than to give the sacrifice of fools: for they consider not that they do evil. 2 Be not rash with thy mouth, and let not thine heart be hasty to utter any thing before God: for God is in heaven, and thou upon earth: therefore let thy words be few. 3 For a dream cometh through the multitude of business; and a fool's voice is known by multitude of words.

5.1-3 Empty religion. Solomon turns his eye to religion. The *hebel* of religion. Jesus also dealt with these issues, mainly the lack of hearing. Jesus said in Mk 8.18 *having ears, ye hear not*. Many passages reflect the lack of hearing by religious people. Jeremiah, Ezekiel, and Isaiah all speak of this perennial problem. Here Solomon also addresses this problem. The eyes and the ears are an integral part of religion. What you speak and look at, as well as what you absorb into your spirit by sight and hearing determine your spiritual status. It is expedient for people to remove any evil from their sight and hearing. Evil is presented on television, Hollywood movies, modern novels, Internet sites, and other platforms. A Christian must keep their home and mind free of this input of evil. Solomon reminds us here, God sees what we watch and listen to. He then adds the second warning about how we speak. This too can be evil. We must be cautious about evil communications. New Testament writers affirm this for the Christian.

5.4-7 When thou vowest a vow unto God, defer not to pay it; for he hath no pleasure in fools: pay that which thou hast vowed. 5 Better is it that thou shouldest not vow, than that thou shouldest vow and not pay. 6 Suffer not thy mouth to cause thy flesh to sin; neither say thou before the angel, that it was an error: wherefore should God be angry at thy voice, and destroy the work of thine hands}? 7 For in the multitude of dreams and many words there are also divers vanities: but fear thou God.

5.4-7 Vows. God expects sincere worship and words from his children. Foolish vows should never be made to God. To not pay our vows to God identifies us as a fool. It is simple; *pay that which thou has vowed*. Be cautious before you make a vow, but once you make it, pay the vow. It is better not to vow at all than to not keep your vows to God.

5.8-9 If thou seest the oppression of the poor, and violent perverting of judgment and justice in a province, marvel not at the matter: for he that is higher than the highest regardeth; and there be higher than they. 9 Moreover the profit of the earth is for all: the king himself is served by the field.

5.8-9 Government. The roaming mental eye of Solomon is viewing all of life. He turns from religion to government. This may be the least surprising *hebel* of life. The only consolation would be, even government officials have authority over them. Even Kings are subject to a higher power.

5.10-12 He that loveth silver shall not be satisfied with silver; nor he that loveth abundance with increase: this is also vanity. 11 When goods increase, they are increased that eat them: and what good is there to the owners thereof, saving the beholding of them with their eyes? 12 The sleep of a labouring man is sweet, whether he eat little or much: but the abundance of the rich will not suffer him to sleep.

5.10-12 Goods. Even the accrual of goods is *hebel*. He that gets silver wants more. Abundance does not bring contentment. Solomon can attest to this, and feels people need to see this *hebel* or vanity of goods and abundance. Abundance of goods can actually rob a man of sleep, while the poor sleep with no worry or care. It is the drive for wealth that does not satisfy man. Solomon's descendant, Jesus Christ, centuries later reaffirms the same conclusion. Luke 12:15; *And he said unto them, Take heed, and beware of covetousness: for a man's life consisteth not in the abundance of the things which he possesseth.*

5.13-17 There is a sore evil which I have seen under the sun, namely, riches kept for the owners thereof to their hurt. 14 But those riches perish by evil travail: and he begetteth a son, and there is nothing in his hand. 15 As he came forth of his mother's womb, naked shall he return to go as he came, and shall take nothing of his labour, which he may carry away in his hand. 16 And this also is a sore evil, that in all points as he came, so shall he go: and what profit hath he that hath laboured for the wind? 17 All his days also

he eateth in darkness, and he hath much sorrow and wrath with his sickness.

5.13-17 Wealth. Wealth is easily lost and not a sure foundation for life. He observes no one takes wealth with them past the grave. He states all this is a sore evil (16), a rubbed and worn sad conclusion to life.

5.18-20 Behold that which I have seen: it is good and comely for one to eat and to drink, and to enjoy the good of all his labour that he taketh under the sun all the days of his life, which God giveth him: for it is his portion. 19 Every man also to whom God hath given riches and wealth, and hath given him power to eat thereof, and to take his portion, and to rejoice in his labour; this is the gift of God. 20 For he shall not much remember the days of his life; because God answereth him in the joy of his heart.

5.18-20 Joy of life. Solomon returns to his theme of the *hebel* of life. He again asserts it is good to eat, drink, and enjoy life. Man is to enjoy his hard work and realize his goods and wealth are a gift from God. A modern day saying would say it this way, "stop and smell the roses."Solomon is confessing he pushed so hard, to achieve so many things; he missed an important facet of life. Life is designed by God to be enjoyed. Solomon repeatedly says, this is the gift of God. Three thousand years have not tarnished this advice. It is still the greatest advice given to mortal man. Life is a gift from God, enjoy it.

Chapter 6

6.1-2 There is an evil which I have seen under the sun, and it is common among men: 2 A man to whom God hath given riches, wealth, and honour, so that he wanteth nothing for his soul of all that he desireth, yet God giveth him not power to eat thereof, but a stranger eateth it: this is vanity, and it is an evil disease.

6.1-2. Prosperity. Prosperity is not always good. Some people lose their spiritual drive when they are blessed with prosperity. Solomon has learned that if you do not keep your spiritual man active toward God, then prosperity can actually be an evil in your life.

6.3-6 If a man beget an hundred children, and live many years, so that the days of his years be many, and his soul be not filled with good, and also that he have no burial; I say, that an untimely birth is better than he. 4 For he cometh in with vanity, and departeth in darkness, and his name shall be covered with darkness. 5 Moreover he hath not seen the sun, nor known any thing: this hath more rest than the other. 6 Yea, though he live a thousand years twice told, yet hath he seen no good: do not all go to one place?

6.3-6 Ibid. He continues to underscore the importance of the spiritual health above all things. To live and be lost is worse than never living at all. The quality of life continues to be his theme. Life is a gift from God, is the canopy he continues to present. The arrival at the grave and the afterlife seem to mesmerize Solomon. It seems as though he cannot shake the unknown after a lifetime of learning about all of life. The moment of death and beyond seem to haunt him with it's unknown. He circles this moment of unease in his writings again and again. He states what he does know. Life here is to be lived and enjoyed. If you live thousands of years and miss this concept, you have failed.

6.7-9 All the labour of man is for his mouth, and yet the appetite is not filled. 8 For what hath the wise more than the fool? what hath the poor, that knoweth to walk before the living? 9 Better is the sight of the eyes than the wandering of the desire: this is also vanity and vexation of spirit.

6.7-9 Ibid. Solomon presents a telling point. In the things that matter most, wealth is not an advantage. The fool has the ability to enjoy food as much as the wealthiest man on earth. It is best to enjoy what you have in the present life, rather than dwell on the wandering desire of the future. To sacrifice present satisfaction to the altar of wishful future things is *hebel*, vanity.

6.10-12 That which hath been is named already, and it is known that it is man: neither may he contend with him that is mightier than he. 11 Seeing there be many things that increase vanity, what is man the better? 12 For who knoweth what is good for man in this life, all the days of his vain life which he spendeth as a

shadow? for who can tell a man what shall be after him under the sun?

6.10-12 The cycle of life. Solomon returns to the cycle of life to illustrate the *hebel* of life. This is a keynote of *hebel*. Man is too limited to explain all the problems of life. The term "who knoweth" is used four times in Ecclesiastes. This is further supported by the seven times Solomon says, "man does not know." After a lifetime of seeking knowledge in all areas of life, the *hebel* of life is we still do not know all things. This is why man is encouraged to enjoy the gift of life while it is available. Life is a shadow, ever changing, ever inching toward the unknown life after death. This is true *hebel*.

Chapter 7

7.1-10 A good name is better than precious ointment; and the day of death than the day of one's birth. 2 It is better to go to the house of mourning, than to go to the house of feasting: for that is the end of all men; and the living will lay it to his heart. 3 Sorrow is better than laughter: for by the sadness of the countenance the heart is made better. 4 The heart of the wise is in the house of mourning; but the heart of fools is in the house of mirth. 5 It is better to hear the rebuke of the wise, than for a man to hear the song of fools. 6 For as the crackling of thorns under a pot, so is the laughter of the fool: this also is vanity. 7 Surely oppression maketh a wise man mad; and a gift destroyeth the heart. 8 Better is the end of a thing than the beginning thereof: and the patient in spirit is better than the proud in spirit. 9 Be not hasty in thy spirit to be angry: for anger resteth in the bosom of fools. 10 Say not thou, What is the cause that the former days were better than these? for thou dost not enquire wisely concerning this.

7.1-10 Good name. A good name proves the presence of wisdom. It is the principals of wisdom that give foundation to a good reputation. The day of death proves our legacy, while the day of birth proves nothing. The house of mourning reminds us of our appointment with God, while laughter makes us forget the present and past. Sorrow makes a man reflect on the brevity of life, therefore it is better. The house of mirth and the laughter of fools is like the crackling of thorns. Solomon is reiterating some of the concepts he wrote in Proverbs. The end of a matter is always better than the beginning. A patient spirit serves better than a proud spirit, for who knows the end of the matter. Anger is true *hebel*, and to live in the past throws today away. This is a violation of the principal of enjoy life and enjoy today. All yesterdays are gone, never to return, and steal today's joy when brooded upon.

7.11-18 Wisdom is good with an inheritance: and by it there is profit to them that see the sun. 12 For wisdom is a defence, and money is a defence: but the excellency of knowledge is, that wisdom giveth life to them that have it. 13 Consider the work of God: for who can make that straight, which he hath made crooked? 14 In the day of prosperity be joyful, but in the day of adversity consider: God also hath set the one over against the other, to the end that man should find nothing after him. 15 All things have I seen in the days of my vanity: there is a just man that perisheth in his righteousness, and there is a wicked man that prolongeth his life in his wickedness. 16 Be not righteous over much; neither make thyself over wise: why shouldest thou destroy thyself? 17 Be not over much wicked, neither be thou foolish: why shouldest thou die before thy time? 18 It is good that thou shouldest take hold of this; yea, also from this withdraw not thine hand: for he that feareth God shall come forth of them all.

7.11-18 Wisdom and life. It is wisdom that brings profit to an inheritance, not the money itself. Riches without wisdom is an evil or *hebel* in itself. With wisdom, money is a defense. Wisdom brings happiness in the day of prosperity and the in the day of adversity. The rise and fall of daily emotions can be trusted to wisdom. Wisdom reveals good days are set against bad days by God himself. Wisdom smoothes out life and gives stability to all seasons, high and low. Solomon muses over the just man who perishes in his righteousness, and the wicked man whose life is prolonged. Without wisdom these life conundrums are troublesome. Solomon advises to not be self-righteous, or seek to be overly wise. This violates the enjoy life as a gift of God concept he is repeatedly presenting. Do not seek evil, but hold in check your wicked nature. The answer is to live, participate in life, while fearing God. This life formula will bring people through any circumstance.

7.19-29 Wisdom strengtheneth the wise more than ten mighty men which are in the city. 20 For there is not a just man upon earth, that doeth good, and sinneth not. 21 Also take no heed unto all words that are spoken; lest thou hear thy servant curse thee: 22 For oftentimes also thine own heart knoweth that thou thyself likewise hast cursed others. 23 All this have I proved by wisdom: I said, I will be wise; but it was far from me. 24 That which is far off, and exceeding deep, who can find it out? 25 I applied mine heart to know, and to search, and to seek out wisdom, and the reason of things, and to know the wickedness of folly, even of foolishness and madness: 26 And I find more bitter than death the woman, whose heart is snares and nets, and her hands as bands: whoso pleaseth God shall escape from her; but the sinner shall be taken by

her. 27 Behold, this have I found, saith the preacher, counting one by one, to find out the account: 28 Which yet my soul seeketh, but I find not: one man among a thousand have I found; but a woman among all those have I not found. 29 Lo, this only have I found, that God hath made man upright; but they have sought out many inventions.

7.19-29 Wisdom and sin. Solomon does not overlook the nature of even good men sinning. The Apostle Paul says in Romans 3.23 *all have sinned*. This is reflected here in Solomon's caveat. The inclusiveness of sin includes words spoken by a person, and spoken of a person, by others. Solomon readily admits he gave himself to seek wisdom and the reason of things. He searched for meaning in sin, folly, and madness. The revolving cycle brought him back to *hebel*, vanity. In his search he saw the bitterness of a woman's snares. As he counted one by one, there was not one man in a thousand who did not sin. The only life worth living is the life of wisdom. Wisdom smoothes out life. Wisdom medicates life. Wisdom intensifies life and it's joy. Wisdom mellows life. Wisdom is the greatest gift of God to make life enjoyable. The highest quality of life is delivered by wisdom. Fear God and embrace wisdom. This is the only alternative to *hebel*.

Chapter 8

8.1 Who is as the wise man? and who knoweth the interpretation of a thing? a man's wisdom maketh his face to shine, and the boldness of his face shall be changed.

8.1 Inner happiness. Solomon was the wisest man to ever live. He has said he sought to know all things. After wasting many years in pursuit of knowledge, he wants to leave succeeding generations the wisdom to not over pursue anything. Enjoy life, and have balance. He concludes that wisdom gives an inner happiness that makes a man's face to shine and his boldness and confidence will be noticeable.

8.2-4 I counsel thee to keep the king's commandment, and that in regard of the oath of God. 3 Be not hasty to go out of his sight: stand not in an evil thing; for he doeth whatsoever pleaseth him. 4 Where the word of a king is, there is power: and who may say unto him, What doest thou?

8.2-4 Kings. The value of wisdom is also on display when in the presence of a king. People were required to take an oath of loyalty to the King when in the King's presence. Wisdom protects people in the presence of all-powerful men who can issue harmful edicts.

8.5-8 Whoso keepeth the commandment shall feel no evil thing: and a wise man's heart discerneth both time and judgment. 6 Because to every purpose there is time and judgment, therefore the misery of man is great upon him. 7 For he knoweth not that which shall be: for who can tell him when it shall be? 8 There is no man that hath power over the spirit to retain the spirit; neither hath he power in the day of death: and there is no discharge in that war; neither shall wickedness deliver those that are given to it.

8.5-8 Time and judgment. Only the wise can discern time, for the tomorrows of life are unknown. Man cannot restrain the spirit, or control the day of death, or be released from war, or be free from wickedness, once it has a hold on him. These four areas of life document that man is limited in his dominion over life. Wisdom shines like a pearl on black velvet when placed next to the powerful entities of life. Without wisdom to teach time and judgment, life dissolves into *hebel*.

8.9-14 All this have I seen, and applied my heart unto every work that is done under the sun: there is a time wherein one man ruleth over another to his own hurt. 10 And so I saw the wicked buried, who had come and gone from the place of the holy, and they were forgotten in the city where they had so done: this is also vanity. 11 Because sentence against an evil work is not executed speedily, therefore the heart of the sons of men is fully set in them to do evil. 12 Though a sinner do evil an hundred times, and his days be prolonged, yet surely I know that it shall be well with

them that fear God, which fear before him: 13 But it shall not be well with the wicked, neither shall he prolong his days, which are as a shadow; because he feareth not before God. 14 There is a vanity which is done upon the earth; that there be just men, unto whom it happeneth according to the work of the wicked; again, there be wicked men, to whom it happeneth according to the work of the righteous: I said that this also is vanity.

8.9-14 Fear God. Solomon here defends the fear of God. He has observed that evil men receive honorable burials and are even praised at death. He observes that sometimes the fortunes of the righteous and the wicked seem to be reversed. The righteous get what the evil deserve, and the evil get what the righteous deserve. Solomon never surrenders to this dilemma. He maintains his strong position to believe in the fear of God. He knows it will go well with them that fear God (12). He knows it will not go well with the wicked (13). This and other passages show Solomon is not an old, bitter, frustrated man. He is clear eyed and has seen life in its fullness. He is seeing through the distortions of life and clearly seeing that no matter how it looks right now, no matter what evidence seems to point toward *hebel*, remember to fear God.

8.15-17 Then I commended mirth, because a man hath no better thing under the sun, than to eat, and to drink, and to be merry: for that shall abide with him of his labour the days of his life, which God giveth him under the sun. 16 When I applied mine heart to know wisdom, and to see the business that is done upon the earth: (for also there is that neither day nor night seeth sleep with his eyes:) 17 Then I beheld

all the work of God, that a man cannot find out the work that is done under the sun: because though a man labour to seek it out, yet he shall not find it; yea farther; though a wise man think to know it, yet shall he not be able to find it.

8.15-17 Mirth. Mirth: exceeding gladness, joy, pleasure, rejoicing. Solomon commends mirth. Commend is to address in a loud tone, to glory, to praise. When faced with the dilemmas and contradictions of life, Solomon says mirth is the answer to confusion and disappointment. Man cannot find out the work done under the sun. Solomon proclaims you can spend a lifetime wondering why someone else is blessed, or you have not gotten your desires. This is futile. It is *hebel* to try and understand hebel. Solomon spent many sleepless nights trying to understand *hebel* (16). His conclusion is to scream with joy and gladness over the joy of today. The answer to the frustrations of life and *hebel* is to praise and glorify God with exceeding gladness. Mirth is the master of *hebel*.

Chapter 9

9.1-6 For all this I considered in my heart even to declare all this, that the righteous, and the wise, and their works, are in the hand of God: no man knoweth either love or hatred by all that is before them. 2 All things come alike to all: there is one event to the righteous, and to the wicked; to the good and to the clean, and to the unclean; to him that sacrificeth, and to him that sacrificeth not: as is the good, so is the sinner; and he that sweareth, as he that feareth an oath. 3 This is an evil among all things that are done under the sun, that there is one event unto all: yea, also the heart of the sons of men is full of evil, and madness is in their heart while they live, and after that they go to the dead. 4 For to him that is joined to all the living there is hope: for a living dog is better than a dead lion. 5 For the living know that they shall die: but the dead know not any thing, neither have they any more a reward; for the memory of them is forgotten. 6 Also their love, and their hatred, and their envy, is now perished; neither have they any more a portion for ever in any thing that is done under the sun.

9.1-6 Death. Solomon addresses the *hebel* of death. Of all the musings and contemplations of Solomon, death is the greatest challenge. Death is unknown and knowledge after death is beyond wisdom to plumb it's depth. There are none to discuss death who have been there and returned. There is a void and a chasm that cannot be crossed. Death is the truest of all *hebels*. The only solution Solomon offers is to stay alive. He surmises any life is better than death. Solomon illustrates this by saying a living dog (despised animal), is better than a dead lion (king of beasts). Ultimately, the search for understanding of *hebel* ends with death. As long as there is life, there is new understanding, knowledge and reward. Life offers continued activity on earth. Life on earth is the only arena of opportunity to accomplish and earn rewards. The grave receives more than the natural body. It also receives dreams, love, hatred, and envy (6). These things also die with the physical body. Many noble but intangible things die with death. Death is the truest of *hebels*. There is no escape or defense from death. It eventually welcomes the righteous, the wise, the wicked, the good, the clean, the unclean, and all other men into its gaping mouth.

9.7-10 Go thy way, eat thy bread with joy, and drink thy wine with a merry heart; for God now accepteth thy works. 8 Let thy garments be always white; and let thy head lack no ointment. 9 Live joyfully with the wife whom thou lovest all the days of the life of thy vanity, which he hath given thee under the sun, all the days of thy vanity: for that is thy portion in this life, and in thy labour which thou takest under the sun. 10 Whatsoever thy hand findeth to do, do it with thy might; for there is no work, nor device, nor knowledge, nor wisdom, in the grave, whither thou goest.

9.7-10 Love. With the wisp of death hanging in the air, Solomon advises to love your wife. While peering into the unknown he is brought back to what he does have now, here. He returns to the God given answer for *hebel*. Live joyfully (with a raw appetite) with the wife of whom thou lovest. That is the portion, (the smoothness), of this life. Thy labor (worry, wearing effort of body and mind) is smoothed out by living life today. Solomon uses words like life, eat, drink, and live. These are actions every person can do. The gift of life God gave requires no wealth or wisdom. The simple man can do these things as well as the wise. God accepteth (is pleased), with these works (actions). God approves when we enjoy life. White garments and oil on the head speak of a more comfortable life in the torrid Middle East climate. These things symbolize the pure enjoyment of a well-lived life, following the guidance of wisdom, and the fear of God.

9.11-18 I returned, and saw under the sun, that the race is not to the swift, nor the battle to the strong, neither yet bread to the wise, nor yet riches to men of understanding, nor yet favour to men of skill; but time and chance happeneth to them all. 12 For man also knoweth not his time: as the fishes that are taken in an evil net, and as the birds that are caught in the snare; so are the sons of men snared in an evil time, when it falleth suddenly upon them. 13 This wisdom have I seen also under the sun, and it seemed great unto me: 14 There was a little city, and few men within it; and there came a great king against it, and besieged it, and built great bulwarks against it: 15 Now there was found in it a poor wise man, and he by his wisdom delivered the city; yet no man remembered that same poor man. 16 Then said I, Wisdom is better

than strength: nevertheless the poor man's wisdom is despised, and his words are not heard. 17 The words of wise men are heard in quiet more than the cry of him that ruleth among fools. 18 Wisdom is better than weapons of war: but one sinner destroyeth much good.

9.11-18 Value of wisdom. The tragedy of life is men are so busy seeking they never see. The value of wisdom is overlooked. Men are as fishes caught in a net, and as birds caught in a snare. The race, the battle, bread, and riches are unpredictable. Our reaction to these is the essence of *hebel*. We cannot control the variables of our lives, but with wisdom and the fear of God, *hebel* fades to insignificance. Solomon illustrates that Kings conquering cities is inferior to wisdom's influence. Wisdom exceeds strength in value. Wisdom is better than weapons of war. The *hebel* of our life results when wisdom is not heard and followed. Death, love, and war, are battlefields of *hebel*. God's victory to these battles is the gift of living life by wisdom, and the fear of God. The vanity of life disappears in the presence of a life of joy and religious celebration.

Chapter 10

10.1-4 Dead flies cause the ointment of the apothecary to send forth a stinking savour: so doth a little folly him that is in reputation for wisdom and honour. 2 A wise man's heart is at his right hand; but a fool's heart at his left. 3 Yea also, when he that is a fool walketh by the way, his wisdom faileth him, and he saith to every one that he is a fool. 4 If the spirit of the ruler rise up against thee, leave not thy place; for yielding pacifieth great offences.

10.1-4 Folly. Folly and foolishness are the opposite of wisdom. A fly in your beverage results in the entire beverage being thrown away. So foolishness in the life of a wise man causes people to dismiss him, and discard him as a valuable man. People realize stupid actions reflect stupid thinking. It is obvious where his heart (desires) is. People say, "There goes the fool." All because of a fly. The text suggests anger is possibly the fly Solomon was mentally seeing. Solomon instructs a calm spirit will bring the best results to conflict. Intemperate people are not considered wise. We see a fly when we view them.

10.5-10 There is an evil which I have seen under the sun, as an error which proceedeth from the ruler: 6 Folly is set in great dignity, and the rich sit in low place. 7 I have seen servants upon horses, and princes walking as servants upon the earth. 8 He that diggeth a pit shall fall into it; and whoso breaketh an hedge, a serpent shall bite him. 9 Whoso removeth stones shall be hurt therewith; and he that cleaveth wood shall be endangered thereby. 10 If the iron be blunt, and he do not whet the edge, then must he put to more strength: but wisdom is profitable to direct.

10.5-10 Ibid. Folly blames failure and mistakes on the leader without investigating the cause. Folly is always immature in its conclusions. Folly places unproven people in elevated positions, while demoting the ones who should be promoted. Men are most often snared by the traps they set themselves. Poetic justice is seen throughout the scriptures. Solomon's father David wrote in 2 Sam 22.27 *with the froward thou wilt show thyself unsavory.* Unsavory means to be twisted. Folly leads a man to be twisted and dishonest, and men who follow this path fall into their own pit they dig. Working with stones and forests can be hazardous, so use wisdom and be careful. A dull ax causes harder work. The investigator of *hebel* is advising to use your head and brains. Wisdom makes labor and life easier, folly defeats in every way.

10.11-15 Surely the serpent will bite without enchantment; and a babbler is no better. 12 The words of a wise man's mouth are gracious; but the lips of a fool will swallow up himself. 13 The beginning of the words of his mouth is foolishness: and the end of his talk is mischievous madness. 14 A fool also is full

of words: a man cannot tell what shall be; and what shall be after him, who can tell him? 15 The labour of the foolish wearieth every one of them, because he knoweth not how to go to the city.

10.11-15 Words. The bite of a serpent is quick and unprovoked. Life lived on Folly Lane will do the same. The babbler (master) is no better. Solomon introduces words verses wisdom. Words from a wise man are beautiful while the fool swallows (destroys) himself. Fools begin with nonsense and end up speaking madness (folly). Here the word folly is used and translated madness. Folly is truly madness. Solomon is cataloging the list of *hebel* produced by folly. It is the cause and effect of folly. A fool is full (multiplies) of words. It is as though the only way he could have said less is to talk more. Foolish talk makes everyone around them tired and the fool cannot find the city (protected place). Fools talk themselves right out of safety.

10.16-20 Woe to thee, O land, when thy king is a child, and thy princes eat in the morning! 17 Blessed art thou, O land, when thy king is the son of nobles, and thy princes eat in due season, for strength, and not for drunkenness! 18 By much slothfulness the building decayeth; and through idleness of the hands the house droppeth through. 19 A feast is made for laughter, and wine maketh merry: but money answereth all things. 20 Curse not the king, no not in thy thought; and curse not the rich in thy bedchamber: for a bird of the air shall carry the voice, and that which hath wings shall tell the matter.

10.16-20 Kings. An unlucky kingdom has a child for a King and this allows the princes to party all night.

Solomon is illustrating the consequences of folly in kings. Blessed is the kingdom where the king is mature and princes (head people, rulers) do not live in folly. The contrast of wisdom and folly in throne rooms is presented. Solomon now leaves the forests and fields and enters the highest places of rulers and laws to show folly is like the spider; it enters King's palaces at times. Verse 18 and 19 almost seem out of place if not viewed in light of the *hebel* of folly in lives of kings. Things put together (building) fall apart without wisdom. Kingdoms cannot rule themselves. A kingdom left unsupervised will decay. While illustrating folly and wisdom as opposites Solomon shows that partying and money are parts of a kingdom. One brings the joy of life and the other provides answers to life needs. Folly speaks against kings out of jealousy or simplicity. Solomon reiterates that the lips of a fool can swallow himself up. If the king hears of your folly (foolish speaking and criticism), the end of the fool is in sight. Folly is the king of *hebel*.

Chapter 11

11.1-6 Cast thy bread upon the waters: for thou shalt find it after many days. 2 Give a portion to seven, and also to eight; for thou knowest not what evil shall be upon the earth. 3 If the clouds be full of rain, they empty themselves upon the earth: and if the tree fall toward the south, or toward the north, in the place where the tree falleth, there it shall be. 4 He that observeth the wind shall not sow; and he that regardeth the clouds shall not reap. 5 As thou knowest not what is the way of the spirit, nor how the bones do grow in the womb of her that is with child: even so thou knowest not the works of God who maketh all. 6 In the morning sow thy seed, and in the evening withhold not thine hand: for thou knowest not whether shall prosper, either this or that, or whether they both shall be alike good.

11.1-6 Employment. One of the arenas of life that *hebel* can rub a person the wrong way is their employment. As one person said, it is so daily. The daily grind of work can become *hebel* very quickly. In these verses, Solomon is instructing about the uncertainty of work. Four times Solomon says, "Thou knoweth not." The encouragement here in reference to our life work is to not give in to the frustrations of *hebel*. The persistent work done daily will bring positive results even if there are moments or extended periods of frustration. The single blow of an ax will not topple an oak tree. The second or third blow may seem pointless. If you continue to strike the oak, eventually it will fall. Solomon is saying keep sowing, ignore the clouds, forget about the wind, just keep working and good things will come to you. This is the formula to conquer *hebel* in your work. Cast your bread (finished product of work), not your seed, upon the waters (life), and somehow it returns in blessing.

11.7-10 Truly the light is sweet, and a pleasant thing it is for the eyes to behold the sun: 8 But if a man live many years, and rejoice in them all; yet let him remember the days of darkness; for they shall be many. All that cometh is vanity. 9 Rejoice, O young man, in thy youth; and let thy heart cheer thee in the days of thy youth, and walk in the ways of thine heart, and in the sight of thine eyes: but know thou, that for all these things God will bring thee into judgment. 10 Therefore remove sorrow from thy heart, and put away evil from thy flesh: for childhood and youth are vanity.

11.7-10 Light and darkness. Solomon is approaching the end of his thoughts on *hebel*. While finishing his thoughts on labor and work he speaks of light and darkness. This is more than light and darkness at face value. Light speaks of illumination and darkness speaks of misery. In the larger picture of *hebel* (vanity), Solomon here uses the imperative mood. He is commanding rather than suggesting. Solomon is strongly admonishing the youth to enjoy life before the onset of feeble years he will address in chapter 12. There will be many days of darkness. There will be days of calamity and defeat. The joy of life will at times not come easy. Solomon is instructing young men to wrestle joy and happiness from life. *Hebel* (vanity), never raises the white flag of surrender. It is work in another profound sense to remove sorrow (vexation, anger) from your heart and evil (adversity, grief, misery), from your flesh. The closing command is to keep working in your natural sense, while continuing to work on the inward hebel that would bring you down and destroy the joy of life. When a man is truly illuminated he will escape the darkness of inner misery. Illumination (light) is the deliverer from *hebel*.

Chapter 12

12.1-8 Remember now thy Creator in the days of thy youth, while the evil days come not, nor the years draw nigh, when thou shalt say, I have no pleasure in them; 2 While the sun, or the light, or the moon, or the stars, be not darkened, nor the clouds return after the rain: 3 In the day when the keepers of the house shall tremble, and the strong men shall bow themselves, and the grinders cease because they are few, and those that look out of the windows be darkened, 4 And the doors shall be shut in the streets, when the sound of the grinding is low, and he shall rise up at the voice of the bird, and all the daughters of musick shall be brought low; 5 Also when they shall be afraid of that which is high, and fears shall be in the way, and the almond tree shall flourish, and the grasshopper shall be a burden, and desire shall fail: because man goeth to his long home, and the mourners go about the streets: 6 Or ever the silver cord be loosed, or the golden bowl be broken, or the pitcher be broken at the fountain, or the wheel broken at the cistern. 7 Then shall the dust return to the earth as it was: and the spirit shall return unto God who gave it. 8 Vanity of vanities, saith the preacher; all is vanity.

12.1-8 Youth and old age. While describing old age,

Solomon is addressing the youthful man. He is warning the young man of what is coming. The darkening of the celestial bodies speaks of declining energy and vitality. The approaching clouds speak of the storms of life and old age. The keepers of the house are the arms, they become feeble and weak. The strong men are the legs that become bowed and weak. The grinders are the teeth that are lost in old age. Those that look out of the window are the eyes and vision fades. Rising at the voice of the bird is loss of sleep. The daughters of music brought low is the loss of hearing. The almond tree is a reference to the white hair of old age. The grasshopper speaks of failed joints that hobble elderly people into painful gaits, limping through their final years. Death is visioned as the shattering of a golden bowl. The pitcher used to hold things from the well (deep things of life), is broken. This is possibly a reference to dementia and memory loss. Solomon paints a realistic picture of life as man approaches the golden years so called. Finally the man himself returns to the original state of dust from which he began. The final cycle of *hebel* has finished it's rotation through life. Through all of this Solomon instructs the young man to always remember his creator, for your creator will be patiently waiting for you when you finish your course.

12.9-11 And moreover, because the preacher was wise, he still taught the people knowledge; yea, he gave good heed, and sought out, and set in order many proverbs. 10 The preacher sought to find out acceptable words: and that which was written was upright, even words of truth. 11 The words of the wise are as goads, and as nails fastened by the masters of assemblies, which are given from one shepherd.

12.9-11 The writer. Solomon describes himself for all future generations. He is not a skeptic or a cynic. He is not an embittered old man. He is acknowledging life as it really is. It is *hebel* to the last day on this earth. He is giving wisdom and acceptable words to balance *hebel*. His words are words of truth. His words are as goads to prod men in life when they are tempted to stop. His proverbs and principals are nails fastened by masters of assemblies (collections of wisdom). This speaks of truths proven on many battlefields of life. Ultimately, These timeless life lessons are from one shepherd, God himself. They are divine instruction on how to live life and enjoy the gift of life from God himself.

12.12-14 And further, by these, my son, be admonished: of making many books there is no end; and much study is a weariness of the flesh. 13 Let us hear the conclusion of the whole matter: Fear God, and keep his commandments: for this is the whole duty of man. 14 For God shall bring every work into judgment, with every secret thing, whether it be good, or whether it be evil.

12.12-14 Conclusion. God has not answered every problem of life. God has commanded man to live joyfully, responsibly, and wisely. The controlling essence of life should be the fear of God. Submit yourself to God and follow the principles he revealed here in Ecclesiastes. This is the best life man can live before the moment he faces God in judgment.

www.ingramcontent.com/pod-product-compliance
Lightning Source LLC
Chambersburg PA
CBHW040326300426
44112CB00021B/2889